THIS JOURNAL
BELONGS TO:

_____

WINE NOTES

a Wine Lover's Journal

tasting tips

Tasting wine should be fun, so enjoy the process of learning to evaluate and describe what you taste as you develop your wine palate. These tips will help you get started.

IN THE GLASS

Appearance
Begin with your eyes as you evaluate a wine's color, hue, clarity, and legs.

Fill a wineglass so that it is about one quarter full. Tilt the glass to a 45 degree angle, hold it up against a white background, and note the intensity of the wine's color. Colors change as wine ages

Different grapes produce wines of different hues. Pale, golden, ruby red: there are many different shades of white and red!

Is the wine cloudy or bubbly? Is it supposed to be? Clarity is important. Some wines are intentionally left unfiltered, but hazy wine may also indicate problems in its production.

Next swirl the wine in the glass. Legs or tears are the drip lines formed as the liquid returns to level. The number of legs goes up with the alcohol content.

Aroma or Bouquet
This is a chance to use your own nose as you describe a wine's "nose."

Swirl the wine in the glass, lean in, and inhale deeply. What do you smell? Would you describe it is fruity or floral? These descriptions are very subjective, and there are many adjectives used to describe a wine's aroma.

IN THE MOUTH

Now the real tasting begins. Swirl a generous teaspoon or so of wine around in your mouth. How does it taste? Is it sweet, sour, acidic, bitter, or just plain wonderful?

If your mouth puckers when tasting a red, the wine may be heavy in tannins—naturally occurring preservatives from grape skins and stems. They are what make red wine so healthy for you.

Once again, pay attention to the wine's aroma. This time, vaporized molecules of the wine go to nasal receptors, and the aroma adds to the sense of a wine's taste.

Does the wine feel light or full on your tongue? This is its viscosity, or body. Is it effervescent? Sparkling wines are traditional for celebrations.

You may note a wine's texture. Is it crisp or soft or smooth? Texture is affected by the wine's acidity and by its alcohol and unfermented sugar content.

A wine's balance means that its component grapes, sugar, acidity, and tannins work together with the body and texture to make a pleasing, balanced whole.

FINISH

Once the wine has been tasted, swallowed, or spat, what's the impression, or finish, it leaves? Describe its character. Perhaps think of what foods it would accompany. Here's your chance to be creative!

Taste, observe, share and drink.

grapes for red wines

BARBERA An Italian grape producing dark, fruity wine.

CABERNET SAUVIGNON Spicy, herby, tannic, with characteris[t] "black currant" aroma. Its wine almost always needs aging. Mak[e] very aromatic rosé.

GAMAY A popular grape in France and Switzerland, used for French Beaujolais and Swiss Dôle.

GRENACHE NOIR A deeply colored grape of southern France a[nd] Italy; used in blends.

MALBEC This French grape produces a strong, dark wine used i[n] Bordeaux and other blended wines.

MERLOT Adaptable grape making fragrant and plummy wines.

MONTEPULCIANO A major Italian grape of high quality.

NEBBIOLO A grape from Italy's Piedmont that ripens during th[e] fogs of late autumn and produces high alcohol wine.

PINOT NOIR The glory of Burgundy's Côte d'Or, with scent, fla[vor] and texture unmatched anywhere.

SANGIOVESE The main red grape of Chianti and much of centr[al] and southern Italy.

SYRAH/SHIRAZ The popular Syrah grape from France is now grown worldwide. Shiraz is the name used for a large variety of Australian wines.

TEMPRANILLO A widely grown Spanish grape used in blends s[uch] as colorful Rioja.

ZINFANDEL Fruity, adaptable grape with blackberry-like, and sometimes metallic, flavor.

grapes for white wines

ALBARIÑO A grape from Galicia, called Alvarinho in Portugal. Sometimes used for Vinho Verde, a fine wine that is drunk young.

BLANC FUME Referring to its reputedly "smoky" smell.

CHARDONNAY Extensively planted world-wide, easy to grow and very versatile.

CHENIN BLANC Can be dry or sweet but with plenty of acidity.

GRÜNER VELTLINER A dry Austrian wine best drunk young. Sometimes used to make Eiswein.

GEWÜRZTRAMINER One of the most pungent grapes, distinctively spicy with aromas like rose petals and cloves.

MUSCAT Possibly the oldest cultivated grape, grown worldwide.

PINOT BLANC Fresh, simple, widely grown grape. Also known as Weissburgunder.

PINOT GRIS/GRIGIO A widely grown grape producing regional varieties of wine ranging from dry to sweet. Pinot Grigio is its crisp Italian iteration.

RIESLING Sensitive to its soil, this grape probably originated along the Rhine and is the most common grape grown in Germany.

SAUVIGNON BLANC Very distinctive aroma of grass or gooseberry; sometimes rank-smelling wines.

SÉMILLON A high yield, resilient grape grown mainly in France and Australia.

VIOGNIER A grape harvested very ripe from the Rhone Valley yielding a high alcohol, fruity, rich textured wine.

wine terms

ACIDITY The amount of acid in the wine: all wine contains acid, but white wine tends to be more acidic than red

AROMA The scent of young wines, not to be confused with bouquet, which is the scent of more mature wines

ASTRINGENT A puckering sensation in the mouth caused by tannins in red wines

ATTACK The first impression of taste

BALANCE Alcohol, fruit, and tannin present in a wine in a harmonious proportion

BEEFY Substantial, sturdy, brawny quality

BITE Perception of tannins and acidity

BODY The weight, texture and alcoholic content of wine

BOUQUET The subtle aroma of a wine, often described fanciful

BRIGHT An impression of visual brilliance especially important for white wines

BUTTERY Refers to a soft, rich vanilla flavor that is characteristi of wines that have been aged in oak casks

CHEWY Wine strong in flavor and high in tannin

CLARITY The appearance of a wine based on the amount of sediment in a wine, ranging from clear through cloudy

CLEAN No impurities in the wine

COARSE Not refined, usually because of the tannin or sparkling wines or large bubbles due to carbonation

COLOR The visual appearance based on chemical compounds the grape's skin. Red wines tend to get paler as they age; white wines increase in color

COMPLEX A desirable quality when many flavors and aromas are individually detectable

CORKY Describes a tainted wine that smells moldy and damp due to a chemical reaction with its cork

CRISP Describes a wine with pleasant acidity

CRUST Sediment on the inside of the wine bottle

DEEP A term sometimes applied to full-flavored wines that have not yet reached their peak

DELICATE Light in flavor and body

DRY Refers to a wine in which most of the sugar content has been fermented into alcohol

EARTHY Usually not complimentary to wines, this term refers to a muddy flavor

FAT A prized quality achieved when weather conditions produce grapes with concentrated flavor and with low acidity

FINISH Sensations perceived after swallowing a wine; aftertaste

FLOWERY The faint scent of flowers, most evident in young or aromatic wines

FRUITY The trace of fruit flavor that can be tasted in certain wines

FULL-BODIED Weighty, substantial wines that are high in alcohol content and generally need time to age

wine terms

GLOSSY Smooth taste of mature red wine

GRAPY The flavor of the grape in the wine

GREEN Unripe, tart taste

HARD A wine that has not been allowed to age sufficiently; contains an excess of tannin

HEADY A wine with a high alcohol content or with a strong aro

HONEYED Ripe white or red wines that have a faint taste of ho

LENGTH The continuation of the wine's flavor in the mouth ev after swallowing

LIGHT-BODIED A wine that is light in flavor and texture and lo in alcohol content

LIVELY Crisp, fresh-tasting wine

MATURE A complex wine that has been allowed to age

MEDIUM-BODIED Between a light-bodied wine and a full-bodi wine in weight, texture and alcohol

NOSE The bouquet or aroma of wine

OAKY A flavor in wines that comes from the oak casks in which it is aged

PALATE Taste and feel of a wine held in the mouth

PLUMMY A characteristic of fully ripe red wines

PRICKLY A slight carbonation perceived in a young, still wine

CH Nice texture and full flavor

PE Natural sweet taste derived from completely ripe grapes

JUND The quality of being mellow with a good body

JUR A taste sensation caused by acids or fermentation

PICY Has the taste of aromatic spices

TRUCTURE Physical constitution of a wine

WEET Describes a wine whose grape sugars have not been completely converted into alcohol

ANNIN The astringent substance found in the seeds and stems grapes and aids in the graceful aging of red wines

ANNIC Contains a lot of tannin; from the skins and pips of apes or from new wooden barrels

JASTY Has the aroma of toasted bread

YPICITY How faithfully a wine represents its varietal grape

ARIETAL A wine made from just one variety of grape

ELVETY A desirably rich, full texture

IVID Making a strong impression on the senses

JLATILE Has a vinegary smell; acetic or pricked

ELL-BALANCED Describes a wine with tannins, alcohol, and Jit in a good proportion

JUNG An immature wine bottled and sold within a year

ONE NOT ONLY

DRINKS WINE

ONE SMELLS IT

OBSERVES

IT

SIPS IT

AND ONE TALKS ABOUT IT

—King Edward VII, English Monarch

Wine

Vintage

date

location

source

price

producer

country/region

grape varieties

color and clarity

aroma/bouquet

body and balance

flavors

Wine	Vintage
date	location
source	price
producer	country/region
grape varieties	
color and clarity	
aroma/bouquet	
body and balance	
flavors	

Wine

Vintage

date

location

source

price

producer

country/region

grape varieties

color and clarity

aroma/bouquet

body and balance

flavors

Wine

Vintage

ate

location

ource

price

roducer

country/region

rape varieties

olor and clarity

roma/bouquet

ody and balance

lavors

Wine   Vintage

date   location

source   price

producer   country/region

grape varieties

color and clarity

aroma/bouquet

body and balance

flavors

Wine

Vintage

date

location

source

price

producer

country/region

grape varieties

color and clarity

aroma / bouquet

body and balance

flavors

Wine   Vintage

date   location

source   price

producer   country/region

grape varieties

color and clarity

aroma / bouquet

body and balance

flavors

Wine	Vintage
date	location
source	price
producer	country/region
grape varieties	
color and clarity	
aroma / bouquet	
body and balance	
flavors	

Wine

Vintage

date

location

source

price

producer

country/region

grape varieties

color and clarity

aroma / bouquet

body and balance

flavors

Wine	Vintage
date	location
source	price
producer	country/region
grape varieties	
color and clarity	
aroma/bouquet	
body and balance	
flavors	

Wine   Vintage

date   location

source   price

producer   country/region

grape varieties

color and clarity

aroma / bouquet

body and balance

flavors

Wine	Vintage
date	location
source	price
producer	country/region
grape varieties	
color and clarity	
aroma/bouquet	
body and balance	
flavors	

Wine	Vintage
date	location
source	price
producer	country/region
grape varieties	
color and clarity	
aroma/bouquet	
body and balance	
flavors	

Wine	Vintage
...ate	location
...urce	price
...oducer	country/region
...ape varieties	
...olor and clarity	
...roma/bouquet	
...dy and balance	
...lavors	

Wine	Vintage
date	location
source	price
producer	country/region
grape varieties	
color and clarity	
aroma/bouquet	
body and balance	
flavors	

Wine	Vintage
date	location
source	price
producer	country/region
grape varieties	
color and clarity	
aroma / bouquet	
body and balance	
flavors	

Wine

Vintage

date

location

source

price

producer

country/region

grape varieties

color and clarity

aroma / bouquet

body and balance

flavors

Wine	Vintage

ate   location

ource   price

roducer   country/region

rape varieties

olor and clarity

roma / bouquet

ody and balance

lavors

Wine

Vintage

date

location

source

price

producer

country/region

grape varieties

color and clarity

aroma/bouquet

body and balance

flavors

Wine

Vintage

ate

location

ource

price

roducer

country/region

rape varieties

olor and clarity

roma/bouquet

dy and balance

lavors

WINE IS

A PASSPORT

to the

WORLD

—Thomas Elkjer

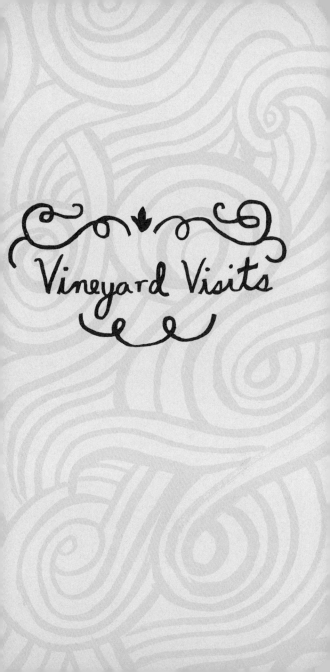

Vineyard Visits

Vineyard   Date

address

phone   website

host

companions

wines tasted

wines purchased   price

1

2

3

4

5

comments

Vineyard _____ Date _____

Address _____

Phone _____ website _____

Cost _____

Companions _____

Wines tasted _____

Wines purchased _____ price _____

Comments _____

Vineyard   Date

address

phone   website

host

companions

wines tasted

wines purchased   price

1

2

3

4

5

comments

Vineyard   Date

Address

Phone   website

Host

Companions

Wines tasted

Wines purchased   price

Comments

Vineyard

Date

address

phone

website

host

companions

wines tasted

wines purchased	price
1	
2	
3	
4	
5	

comments

Vineyard   Date

Address

Phone   website

Cost

Companions

Wines tasted

Wines purchased   price

Comments

Vineyard   Date

address

phone   website

host

companions

wines tasted

wines purchased   price

1

2

3

4

5

comments

Vineyard   Date

Address

Phone   website

host

companions

wines tasted

wines purchased   price

comments

Vineyard   Date

address

phone   website

host

companions

wines tasted

wines purchased   price

1

2

3

4

5

comments

Vineyard

Date

Address

Phone   website

Host

Companions

Wines tasted

Wines purchased   price

Comments

Vineyard

Date

address

phone   website

host

companions

wines tasted

wines purchased	price
1	
2	
3	
4	
5	

comments

Vineyard   Date

Address

Phone   website

Host

Companions

Wines tasted

Wines purchased   price

Comments

Vineyard

Date

address

phone

website

host

companions

wines tasted

wines purchased	price
1	
2	
3	
4	
5	

comments

Vineyard   Date

dress

one   website

st

mpanions

nes tasted

ines purchased   price

mments

Vineyard   Date

address

phone   website

host

companions

wines tasted

wines purchased   price
1
2
3
4
5

comments

ineyard   Date

dress

one   website

st

mpanions

nes tasted

ines purchased   price

mments

Vineyard

Date

address

phone   website

host

companions

wines tasted

wines purchased   price

1

2

3

4

5

comments

Vineyard   Date

Address

Phone   website

Host

Companions

Wines tasted

Wines purchased   price

Comments

Vineyard   Date

address

phone   website

host

companions

wines tasted

wines purchased   price
1
2
3
4
5

comments

Vineyard   Date

Address

Phone   website

Host

Companions

Wines tasted

Wines purchased   price

Comments

WINE IS BOTTLED POETRY

— Robert Louis Stevenson

Notes, Addresses, and Wine Labels

Addresses

wine merchants, wine clubs, vineyards, cellars, organizatio

Addresses

ine merchants, wine clubs, vineyards, cellars, organizations

Addresses

wine merchants, wine clubs, vineyards, cellars, organizatio

Addresses

ine merchants, wine clubs, vineyards, cellars, organizations

Addresses

wine merchants, wine clubs, vineyards, cellars, organizatio

ddresses

ne merchants, wine clubs, vineyards, cellars, organizations

Addresses

wine merchants, wine clubs, vineyards, cellars, organizatio

ddresses

ne merchants, wine clubs, vineyards, cellars, organizations

Wine

Date

Paste Label Here

comments   rating ☆ ☆ ☆ ☆

Wine

_____

Date

_____

Comments   rating ☆ ☆ ☆ ☆ ☆

_____

_____

_____

_____

Wine

Date

Paste Label Here

comments   rating ☆ ☆ ☆ ☆

Wine

Date

Paste Label Here

Comments   rating ☆ ☆ ☆ ☆ ☆

Wine

Date

comments   rating ☆ ☆ ☆ ☆

Wine

Date

Paste Label Here

Comments   rating ☆ ☆ ☆ ☆ ☆

Wine

Date

comments   rating ☆ ☆ ☆ ☆

Wine

Date

Paste Label Here

Comments   rating ☆ ☆ ☆ ☆ ☆

Wine

Date

comments   rating ☆ ☆ ☆ ☆

Wine

Date

Paste Label Here

omments   rating ☆ ☆ ☆ ☆ ☆

Wine

Date

comments   rating ☆ ☆ ☆ ☆

Wine

Date

Paste Label Here

omments   rating ☆☆☆☆☆

Wine

Date

comments   *rating* ☆ ☆ ☆ ☆

Wine

Date

Paste Label Here

Comments   rating ☆ ☆ ☆ ☆ ☆

Wine

Date

comments   rating ☆ ☆ ☆ ☆

Wine

Date

Paste Label Here

omments   rating ☆ ☆ ☆ ☆ ☆

Wine

Date

Paste Label Here

comments   rating ☆ ☆ ☆ ☆

Wine

Date

Paste Label Here

Comments   rating ☆ ☆ ☆ ☆ ☆

Wine

Date

comments   rating ☆ ☆ ☆ ☆

Wine

Date

Comments   rating ☆ ☆ ☆ ☆ ☆

NOTES

NOTES

NOTES

NOTES

NOTES

NOTES

artwork © DANIELLE KROLL
WWW.HELLODANIELLEKROLL.COM
design © GALISON
WWW.GALISON.COM

GALISON
NEW YORK
WWW.GALISON.COM

9H7-F5D-3B1-0
ISBN 978-0-7353-3530-1

9 780735 335301

GALISON 28 WEST 44TH STREET · NEW YORK, NY 10036
Designed in the U.S.A. Manufactured in China